Copyright © 2020 by Rafael J. Rivera-Viruet

All rights reserved. No part of this publication may be reproduced, distributed, or transmitted in any form or by any means, including photocopying, recording, or other electronic or mechanical methods, without the prior written permission of the publisher, except in the case of brief quotations embodied in critical reviews and certain other noncommercial uses permitted by copyright law. For permission requests, write to the publisher, addressed "Attention: Permissions Coordinator," at: rrivera@terramaxent.com

All images in this book are owned by their respective copyright holder and are used under section 107 of the Copyright Act of 1976, for "fair use" for purposes of comment, teaching, scholarship, education and research.

Published by: Terramax Entertainment

Cover design and Pagination by MRCS

Library of Congress Cataloging-in-Publication Data

ISBN 978-0-9816650-1-6

    Rivera-Viruet, Rafael J.

        Dream Chaser

        The Business of Showbiz

Acknowledgements

I would like to thank all the wonderful friends and family who in one way or another contributed to my efforts in writing and securing many of the photos and an invaluable amount of information to share. These individuals include Stephen Sultan, Mitch Douglas, Shelly Schultz, Andy Baltimore, Dr. Andrew Rosen, Rene Lopez, Andy Kaufman, Maggie Viruet, Joseph Rivera, Paul Lichtman and Michael Cooperman.

I thank my fantastic editor, Ronnie Lovler for her sensitive editorial suggestions and creativity. Max Resto, my associate in numerous collaborations, continues to demonstrate his creativeness and I thank him for his edits, the design of the cover and his new media savvy.

Rafael "Ralph" Rivera-Viruet

Rafael J. Rivera-Viruet, A/K/A Ralph Rivera, was born in the central mountains of Puerto Rico on a coffee farm in the town of Utuado. He arrived in New York during the "Great Migration" of the late 1940s to live in the South Bronx. He is a product of the New York City public school system and realized his first dream… "go to college and get out of poverty". With the knowledge that he absorbed and his business savvy, it gave him the opportunity to fulfill the dream of becoming a major Financial Executive and Producer on an international level in the entertainment business.

In the late 1960s, while working for the CPA firm Price Waterhouse, he was recruited by the Ashley Famous Talent Agency and guided the company's financial affairs. As CFO and with his mentor Marvin Josephson, they created mergers and acquisitions to form International Creative Management, (I C M), the Behemoth Talent Agency… dream fulfilled.

In 1980, searching for more dreams, he was offered an opportunity to relocated to Los Angeles to work with Martin Starger (Former President of ABC television) and Sir Lew Grade, the head of the British entertainment company, Marble Arch Productions. Some of the projects that he was involved with include Academy award-winning films "On Golden Pond" and "Sophie's Choice". He then joined Marvel Comics and worked with Stan Lee and Tony Pastor in the television animation productions of "Spider-Man", "Iron Man" and "Fantastic Four" for FOX Children's Television.

He was fortunate to survive an earthquake in 1994, and relocated to San Juan, PR where he began to produce historical documentaries on Hispanic culture. After 9/11, he returned to New York to work with Stephen Sultan, the President of Dramatists Play Service and together they were able to double the company's assets and created the largest licensing and publishing company in American theatre.

I addition to writing his memoirs as a series of ePicture books, he is also the co- author of the Award-winning Reference and Research picture book "Hollywood… Se Habla Español", a 25 years historical research project on contributions made by Hispanics in Hollywood films over the last 100 years. In 2014, he produced the Off-Broadway musical "The Zombies: A Musical Spoof!".

TABLE OF CONTENTS

The Formation of I C M - The Ten Percenters —————————————— 13

Playing with the Numbers ——————————————— 36

London and Joyful Paris ———————————————— 38

Going Public Through the Back Door ——————————— 44

The Art of Movie Packaging ——————————————— 46

The Hiring and Training Practices ————————————— 50

The Towering Inferno —————————————————— 53

The 1976 Summer Olympics ——————————————— 56

Steve McQueen and The 1968 Ford Mustang GT Fastback ————— 60

Visiting Communist Cuba - The Bombing of Lincoln Center - Havana Jam —— 65

The Writing on the Wall - Going to Hollywood - Life is But a Dream ————— 76

Cover Photos from left to right. Top row: Robert Kennedy, Milton Goldman, Still from the Captain Kangoroo TV Show.
Bottom: Ed Limato, Sue Mengers, far right, with Farrah Fawcett and Ryan O'Neal at a party at Studio 54 in New York in September 1981, Andy Baltimore and Larry Rosen.

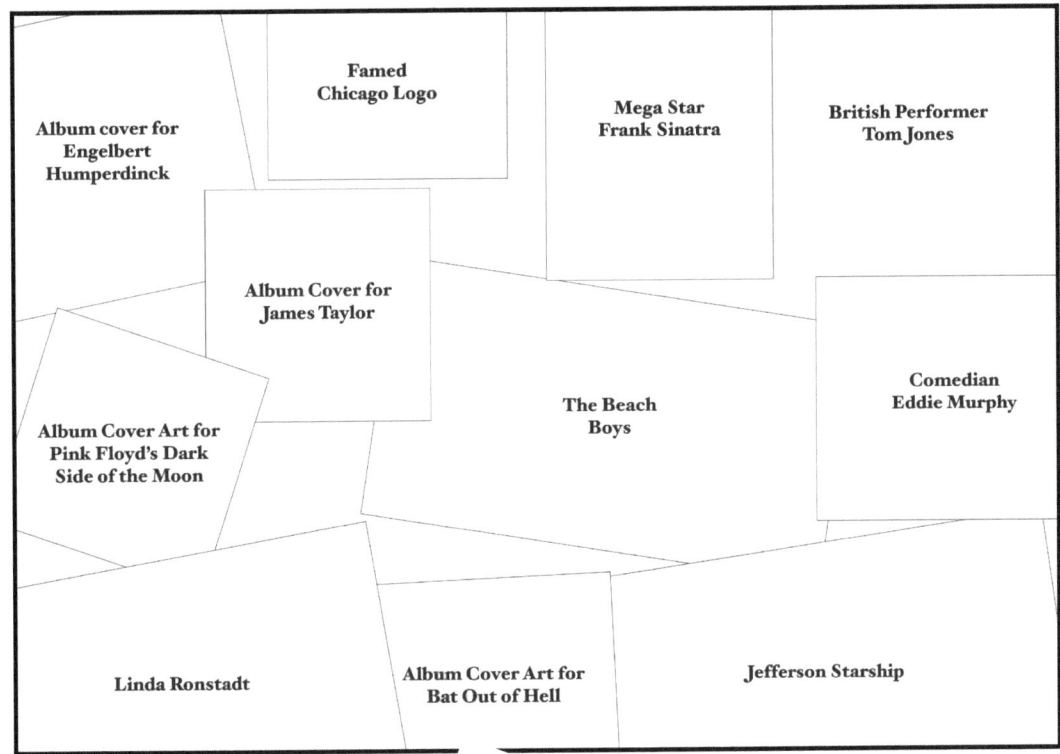

Photo Map pages 28 and 29.

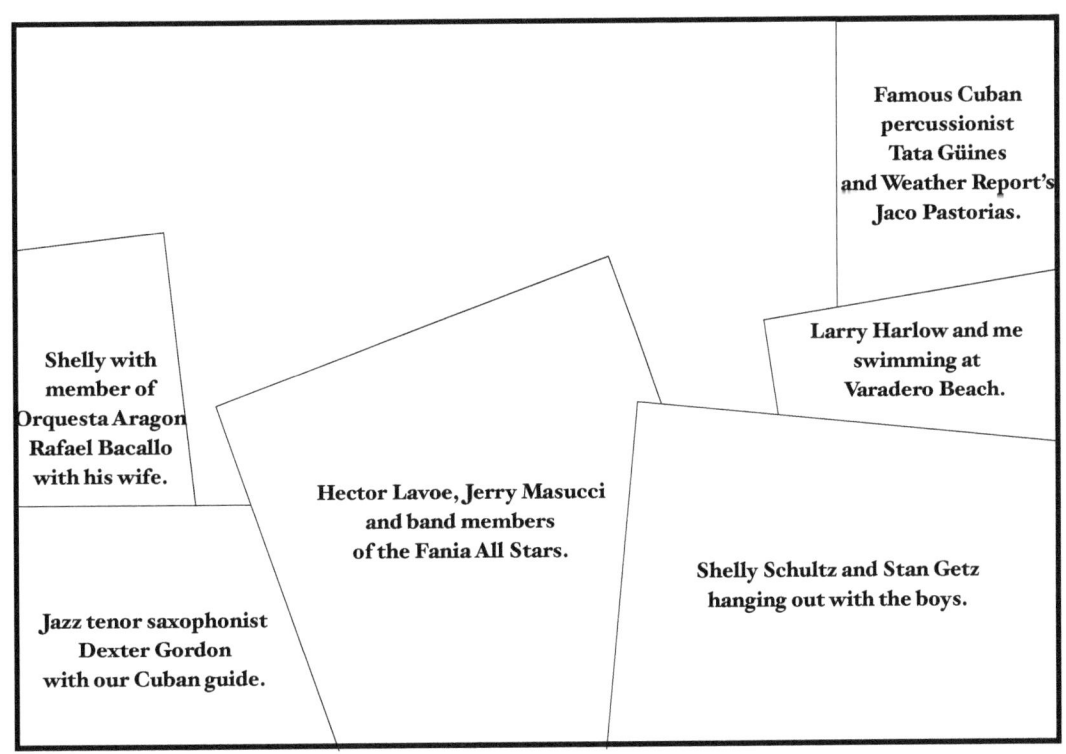

Photo Map pages 74 and 75.

Foreword

Rafael (Ralph) Rivera, has lived the American dream. He made it happen in the Entertainment Business, which is not known for promoting Hispanic business leaders. Ralph's ambition and acumen helped him flourish as a key executive with an international theatrical agency. His professional biography is a primer for anyone interested in the business world in the entertainment industry. Fifty years ago, I met Ralph at the beginning of his career and was happy to participate in just a few of his accomplishments, but more importantly found a fun-loving friend for life.

– Stephen Sultan, Lenox, Mass.

Chapter I

The Formation of ICM - The Ten Percenters

I began the decade of the 1970s excited and felt great about myself leaving the accounting profession and entering into "the business of showbiz." As I prepared to start my new position as Comptroller of Ashley Famous Agency (AFA), I thought, "this opportunity is going to allow me to learn about the production process of movies, television programs, commercials, the Broadway theatre business, the ins and outs of the complicated music industry and the book publishing field." I was just 30 years old and felt like a giant and the luckiest person in the world. With the knowledge that I had gained on creative ideas and methods to make small companies grow and become profitable at the small accounting firm, Curran & Company and at the giant CPA firm, Price Waterhouse, I felt ready for the challenge and said to myself, "bring it on!"

During this fantastic new journey, I got to meet and work with a wide range of some of the most interesting and dynamic people in show business. I'm going to introduce you to them and describe events that occurred from my perspective.

For over two months before joining the company, I met with the head of AFA's New York office, Karl Honeystein, who had also interviewed me. He was an entertainment attorney, a television packaging agent and also my new boss. He gave me insights into the agency's business background and information on the main players at Ashley Famous in New York, Los Angeles, and the company's European offices. Karl was always elegantly dressed, very much a people person and had strong negotiating skills, which was apparent by his success in getting television programs on the air at all three major networks - ABC, CBS, and NBC.

I'm a history buff and will always remember Karl's wonderful stories. He was very specific and detailed, and in listening to him, I was amazed by the way business got done in Hollywood. Agents in the entertainment industry have a major role in obtaining opportunities for their clients,

Ted Ashley, left, chairman of the board and chief executive officer of Warner Bros., and Frank Sinatra, right, present Jack L. Warner with a silver plaque.

and in exchange, they get a 10% commission on all revenues that the clients generate. The Music Corporation of America (MCA), which started as a small band booking agency in Chicago in 1924, developed a booming business during the 1940s, '50s, and '60s. By the early 1960s, they had created a conglomerate that many considered to be a monopoly. They owned and controlled major record labels, a talent agency that controlled the artists, and several film and television production companies. The government's Department of Justice, headed by then Attorney General Robert F. Kennedy came in and let them know they could either keep the talent agency business or the production companies, but not both. MCA's ownership of the production companies was clearly more profitable than the agency business, so the decision was obvious. The talent agency represented most of Hollywood's biggest names and owning the production companies violated antitrust laws. In an earlier case against MCA, the judge called the company "the Octopus… with tentacles reaching out to all phases and grasping everything in show business."

    The breakup of the MCA booking agency business led to the creation of over twenty different talent agencies. One of them was Ashley Famous Agency (AFA), founded by Ted Ashley and his brother Al in 1951, and they benefited greatly by hiring many of the agents that represented the major music, film and television artists at MCA. Together they made the agency a powerful international force. But Ted wanted to go into film production, so they sold AFA to the Kinney National Company in 1967 in exchange for 12,750,000 shares of Warner Bros. stock.

The Kinney National Company was formed by the merger of a parking garage company (Kinney Parking Company) and National Cleaning Contractors, Inc. in 1966. By 1969, Steve Ross, the head of Kinney and an intimate friend of Ted Ashley, had acquired numerous companies including the cash-strapped film production company, Warner Bros.-Seven Arts. Ted Ashley was appointed CEO of the new Warner Bros. and he realized that Kinney had to sell AFA because of the same anti-trust laws that had caused the breakup of MCA.

News of the impending sale reached Marvin Josephson, a lawyer by trade, who started his career at CBS in the contract department but became dissatisfied there because he had no one-on-one contact with clients. He wanted to deal with clients directly, so he left the network to become an independent agent and together with Ralph Mann, formed Marvin Josephson Associates (MJA). They

Marvin Josephson.

established a small but lucrative talent agency that represented well-known newscasters like Harry Reasoner, Tom Brokaw, and the king of children's television programming, Robert Keeshan, popularly known as Captain Kangaroo, whose show was on the air for 15 years at the CBS network . Josephson also saw an opportunity in the book publishing field and established a literary department that represented major authors, including the former Secretary of State, Henry Kissinger and others who were frequently on the New York Times' best-seller lists. His main book agent on staff was Lynn Nesbit, who became one of the most powerful literary agents in the business for decades.

Marvin was a big thinker and his goal was to create a large scale, full-service

Harry Reasoner, above. Below, Henry Kissinger.

Robert Keeshan, popularly known as "Captain Kangaroo."

entertainment conglomerate like everyone else in that business was doing. He knew that Steve Ross and Ted Ashley needed to get rid of AFA, and in 1969 he made an offer to buy the company for $12.5 million, even though he didn't have the money. Marvin once said to me "I had to take a big risk to buy AFA. My company was worth less than $2 million. I put on blinders and went ahead." I asked him how he raised the money? He said, "I went to my rich friends and contacts like bankers, lawyers, insurance company executives and my accountants at Price Waterhouse. I sold them the vision that I had and was able to get the balance of the money. That's why we hired you. To keep our money safe and make it grow." I just smiled and shook my head up and down.

Current photo of Literary agent Lynn Nesbit with Victor Navasky former editor of The Nation Magazine.

Bob Chuck.

A few months later, on January 5, 1970, I joined AFA at 1301 Avenue of the Americas and 52nd Street in Manhattan, close to where all the major television networks were located. Marvin called me from Los Angeles, to welcome me. He was very gracious and told me "if you have a problem with anyone, let me know because we have a lot of work to do, I want to take our company public. I'm looking at about three to five years and when that happens, we are going to issue stock options to all the executives, this will allow us to keep everyone happy." I felt good about our conversation and made my own commitment to grow the company and take it public.

When Marvin acquired AFA, the Hollywood newspapers and gossip columns called it a daring move. The entertainment industry is all about status and prestige; only a few people in the business knew anything about Marvin Josephson. With his purchase of the agency, his name began to appear in the headlines of *Variety, The Hollywood Reporter* and various financial newspapers like *The Wall Street Journal,* describing him as a major deal maker. This was good news and it gave us free publicity that helped to get the word out and continue our forward momentum.

We envisioned ourselves as a strong international entertainment company with offices in New York, Los Angeles, London, and Paris, and with an affiliate in Rome. It now became important to create a new image to reflect the new ownership. Accordingly, we changed the name from Ashley Famous Agency to International Famous Agency (IFA), a subsidiary of Marvin Joseph Associates, Inc.

The hierarchy of MJA, the holding company, was small. Marvin was the chairman of the board and he had dozens of outside advisors. Sometimes I thought it was good and other times not so good. He was always dressed in a suit and tie, trim and fit. He was a loner, who was also very secretive and who did not like to socialize. He was an extremely bright lawyer with great business acumen. To me, he was the ultimate deal-maker but really not an agent. His friend and longtime associate, Ralph Mann, played that role. Ralph wore many hats; new head of all activities in New York, vice chairman of the board of directors of MJA, head of the various music departments and company hatchet man. Ralph always had a great smile and I considered him the real agent in the talent and entertainment business, and therefore, a perfect match for Marvin who lacked those characteristics. The other important member of his inner circle was Bob Chuck, another very smart lawyer, who had worked with Marvin at CBS. Bob played a key role; we all considered him to be Marvin's main confidant, and his duties also included the titles of secretary and treasurer for the corporation. He was a very busy guy and most of the time overwhelmed with so many responsibilities. Muriel Hewitt, Marvin's bookkeeper since he started his company, was also part of the group. Muriel was a sweetheart and very loyal to Marvin. I considered her the hand-holder for all of Marvin's clients, especially the very demanding Bob Keeshan.

Stephen "Steve" Sultan and his wife Judy. Opposite page: The Sultan Family.

The first year of IFA was nothing but turmoil, with too many employees confused about who was really in charge. Bob Chuck now had major responsibilities and everyone, myself included, had to go to him for advice since we all felt that Marvin did not like dealing with day-to-day business and personnel issues. He would come back with solutions that we knew were the results of his conversations with Marvin. Bob worked well with everyone and he gave me opportunities to grow within the company. I always felt that Bob and I would stay friends forever and we supported each other in the political disagreements that exists in the corporate world.

Karl Honeystein was no longer the head of the New York Office. He was now in charge of the business affairs team and television packaging. He was not happy about his new role in the company and he left less than a year later and went to Hollywood to produce television shows. Irwin Moss, who became the new head of business affairs, had a reputation for being hardnosed, but he was a great deal maker. Irwin and I became good friends and worked well together. We were always finding solutions to the internal conflicts that occur when big companies merge. I have wonderful memories of his beautiful rose garden parties each year at the beginning of June in Westchester County. Irwin worked very hard on his rose bushes and they looked beautiful. We kidded around by telling him that his wife Blanche had done a great job and it annoyed him. He would say, "I'm the one who did all the work."

I was lucky to meet an attorney who I considered my brother from our first conversation. We developed a wonderful lifelong friendship. Stephen "Steve" Sultan came from the same crowd of entertainment attorneys who worked at MCA and was a great team player. He was like an encyclopedia of the Broadway theatre business and the world of publishing. We consider him the guru and he was a *mensch* (a Yiddish word for a person of integrity and honor), a fly on the wall, always there; but few knew his contributions to the company. He was responsible for all business matters relating to two departments that were filled with theatre and publishing "divas," and of course he had to deal with all the issues that they frequently caused. These two departments were like having ten to twelve small "boutique agencies," each one very protective of their clients so Stephen and I were always putting out fires. To get rid of our frustrations, our normal ritual was to buy a sandwich at the Jewish Deli on 57th Street and walk to Central Park, six blocks away, find a bench where we could sit, eat, relax, smoke, and talk about our personal lives. He had gone through a difficult divorce and it wore him down. I was not happy at home so we both felt the need to bond as brothers and talk about what was happening in our

Original Poster Art for Grease.

personal lives. He was constantly talking about his beautiful new love, Judy Korman. Steve had a son, Peter, whom Judy loved as if he were her own and he was about the same age as my son, Andy. After we introduced the two kids, they formed a wonderful friendship. We all considered Steve and Judy to be the perfect couple and finally they got married and had a beautiful daughter, Arian. Peter was so excited to have a little sister. They consider me part of their "mishpucha" (family) and I have personally experienced their love of family for nearly fifty years.

Steve had a great taste for live theatre and in 1971, a young music agent invited him to go with him to Chicago to the opening of a musical. When he returned, he called me and said "What are you doing for lunch? I need to speak to you about my trip to Chicago." He sounded excited; he knew my love for music and when he told me about the play and the terrific music, I asked him "What's the title of the show again?" he said "*Grease.*" That's just a small example of Steve's abilities to pick winning Broadway-bound projects.

On one of our walks to Central Park, Steve and I were talking about different types of ethnic foods and he asked me, "What are cuchifritos?" I laughed out loud and said, "They're a type of pork

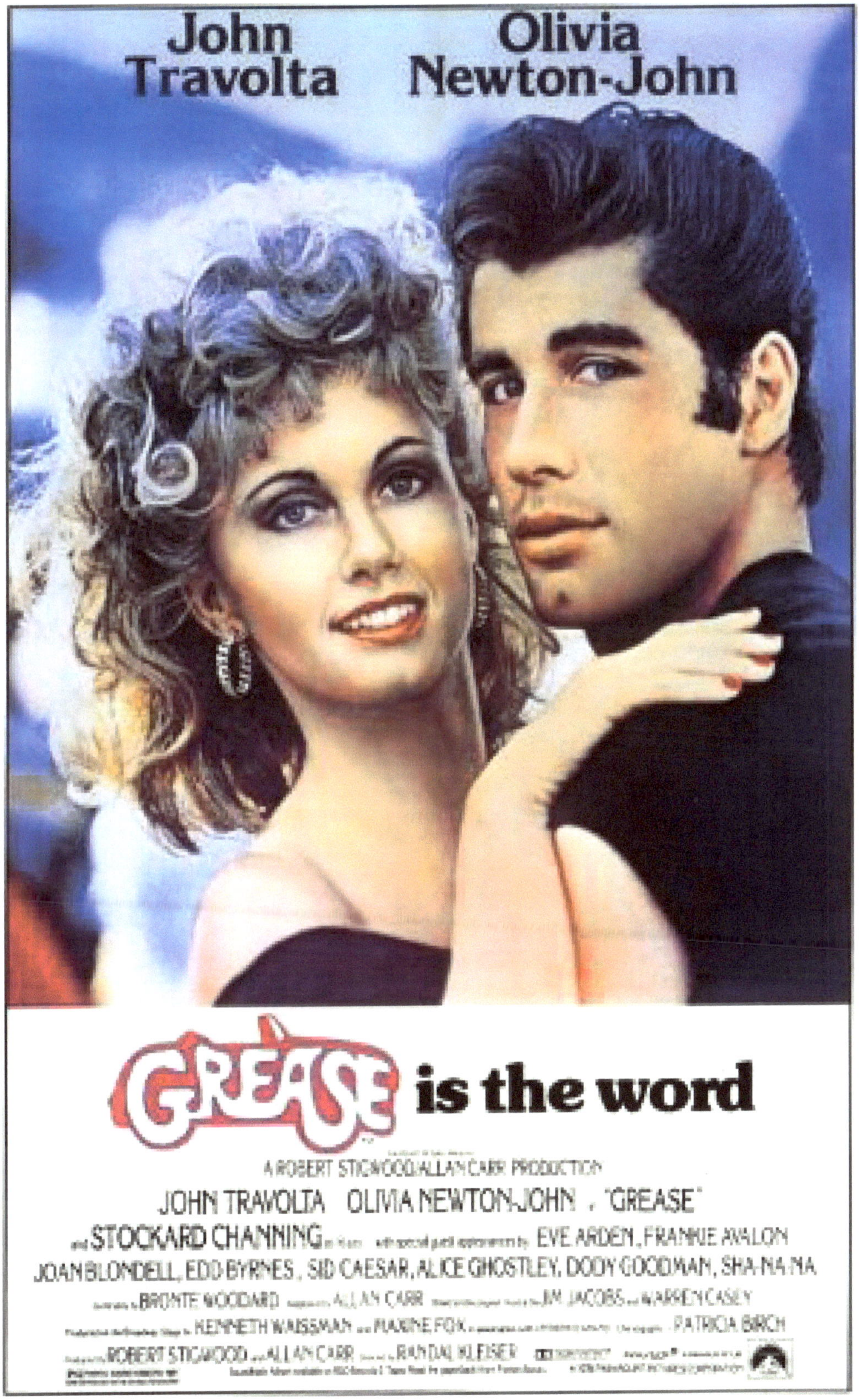
John Travolta
Olivia Newton-John
GREASE is the word
A ROBERT STIGWOOD/ALLAN CARR PRODUCTION
JOHN TRAVOLTA OLIVIA NEWTON-JOHN "GREASE"
STOCKARD CHANNING
EVE ARDEN, FRANKIE AVALON
JOAN BLONDELL, EDD BYRNES, SID CAESAR, ALICE GHOSTLEY, DODY GOODMAN, SHA-NA-NA
BRONTE WOODARD
ALLAN CARR
JIM JACOBS
WARREN CASEY
KENNETH WAISSMAN
MAXINE FOX
PATRICIA BIRCH
ROBERT STIGWOOD
ALLAN CARR
RANDAL KLEISER

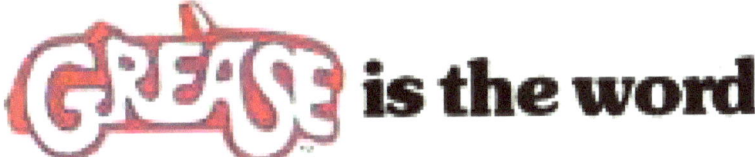

Present day Cuchifritos restaurant in El Barrio.

meat and vegetables made with Puerto Rican condiments and most of the time it is deep fried. Do you want to try some? We can go to El Barrio." Is it safe there he said? I told him that there were many stories, but I never had an issue. We decided to go on a double date, Steve and Judy and me with my friend, Rosalie. We went to the most famous cuchifritos restaurant in El Barrio, on the corner of 110th Street and Lexington Avenue. It was a hot summer evening and I had a car with a sunroof that I opened to get a better view. I parked the car directly across the street and said, "Steve, let's go inside and I'll show what's good and you can look around". We went in to order the food and I gave the server a twenty-dollar bill. We were waiting for the change when suddenly there was a shootout and everyone in the restaurant began to panic. I grabbed my change and yelled out, "Steve! Get down!" We crawled to the door and ran to the car. As we were running to the car we saw Judy and Rosalie with their heads above the sunroof yelling and waving for us to hurry. We are still laughing about the episode, but I must say, it was very scary.

    The office Manager, Arthur Trefe was probably the most important company staff member. He was from a Greek family and was a master at dealing with the staff issues and conflicts that normally come into play when large companies merge. He too had been with all the predecessor companies including MCA and was an encyclopedia of who was who in the business. Arthur was a kind person, but he was not someone to mess with; believe me, you did not want to get on his bad side. He was the main person that everyone came to ask for all sorts of advice, whether it was business related or personal. He was great at handholding and his very funny Irish wife, Elizabeth (Lizzy), made us feel at home. Arthur would always joke by saying that we were all his children. A number of us had a routine, after 6 PM, when most of the staff had gone home. It was then that we would congregate in Arthur's office or his apartment, that was a block away on 56th Street, for cocktails and to listen to jazz and talk about all the rumors in and out of the company.

The television packaging revenues generated by the agents were astronomical. Gary Nardino, Frank Konigsberg, Lee Gabler, Irwin Moss, David Kennedy, and the young energetic Danny Schrier together with Bob Broder in Los Angeles led the way. These agents were very good at what they did, and they knew it. New York was the mecca of the advertising industry and it was all about having the right relationships, so you can imagine all the handholding and conciliatory

Producer Gary Nardino and Actress Barbara Eden.

Television Executive Lee Gabler.

Television Producer David Kennedy.

Music Agent Shelly Schultz

actions taken whenever they requested certain privileges. The other major revenue generator was the Television Commercials department, headed by Peter Kelly. He had an uncanny ability to select talent for voice-over commercials and everyone in the advertising business respected him.

Hanging out with music agents was my favorite thing to do. I looked for ways to travel to concerts with super music agents like Joe Higgins, Shelly Schultz, and Ed Ruben, who represented entertainers like Tom Jones and Engelbert Humperdinck, two of the biggest stars in popular music at the time. Herb Spar headed the Rock & Roll department, with a client list that included some of the world's most famous rock & roll artists of the 1970s, like Grace Slick and Jefferson Starship, The Beach Boys, Chicago and Pink Floyd. I have fond memories of Andy Kaufman, a young music agent and one of Shelly's protégés, who years later became a major Latin music producer. One of my highlights was when Shelly invited me to the green room at Madison Square Garden and introduced me to Frank Sinatra. Shelly was a fun guy to be with, always joyful, with many wonderful stories to tell. His clients adored him and years later he was inducted into the *Rock and Roll Hall of Fame* for his contribution to the industry and guiding his clients to stardom, including artists like iconic folk singer Linda Ronstadt, James Taylor, and Eddie Murphy, just to name a few.

The agency had a group of female agents who had worked for MCA and were considered legends in the theatre and book publishing worlds. I took every opportunity to get to know each and every one, and I was able to work well with them. One of the toughest was Kay Brown; she was very proper, straight to the point and the agent responsible for the success of author Margaret Mitchell, whose 1936 novel *Gone with The Wind*, became an Academy Award-winning film three years later. Kay was not afraid of using four-letter words and she one day said to me "If they don't like it, tough shit." I just stood there and laughed.

Literary agent Katharine "Kay" Brown Barrett

Another interesting personality was Monica McCall, a small British woman, very formal and when I went to her office to meet with her, she would rest her feet under her desk on an embroidered footstool. She represented a blue-chip roster of clients like, Graham Greene, whose written works included *Our Man in Havana* and *The Quiet American*, the French playwright Jean Giraudoux, and John van Druten, whose play *I Am a Camera* eventually became the very popular and profitable Broadway musical *Cabaret*. She was also the agent for the Goldman brothers: Bill, who wrote *Butch Cassidy and the Sundance Kid*, and James, who wrote the play *The Lion in Winter*.

Original 1940 hardcover edition of *Gone With the Wind*.

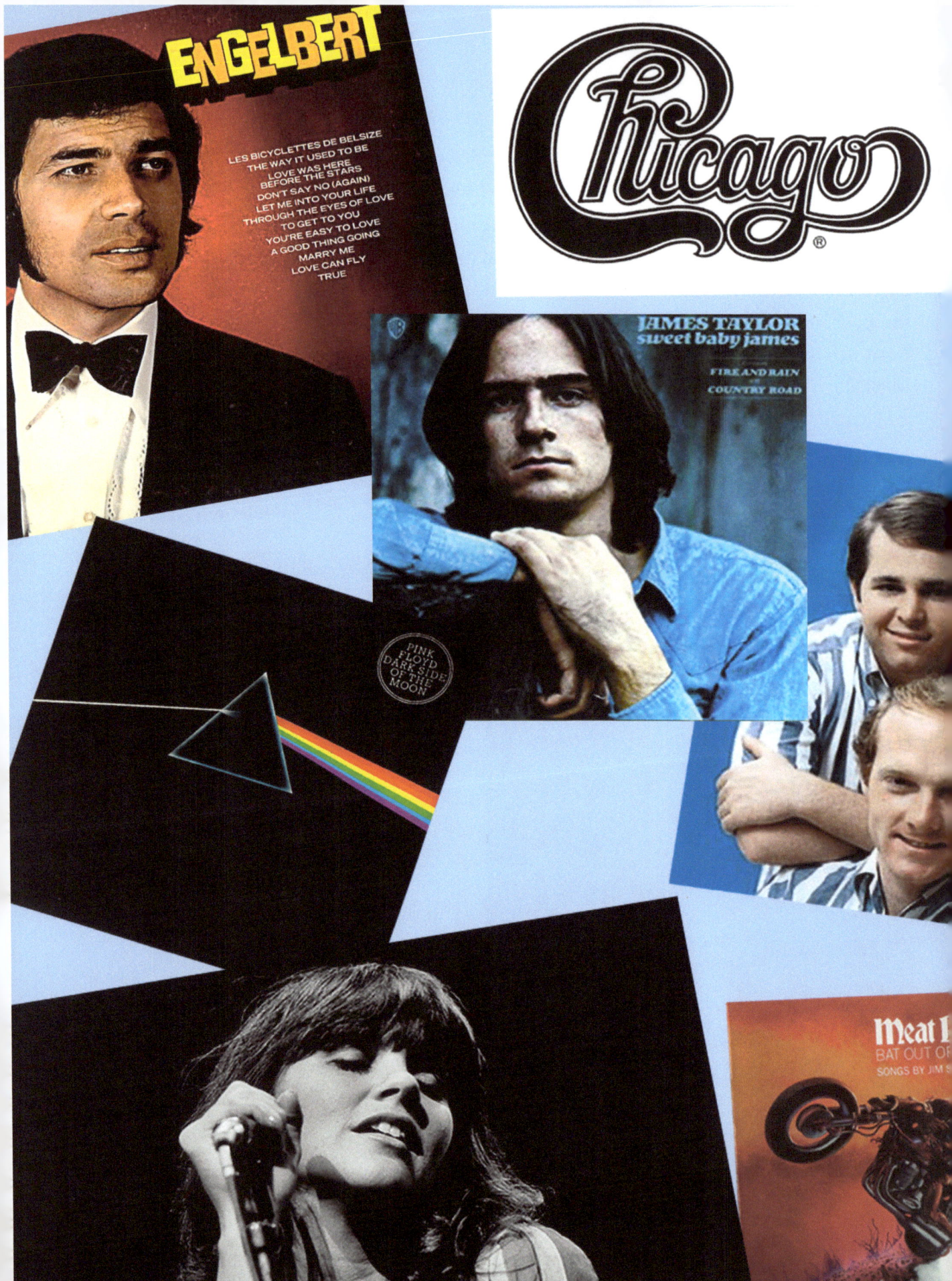

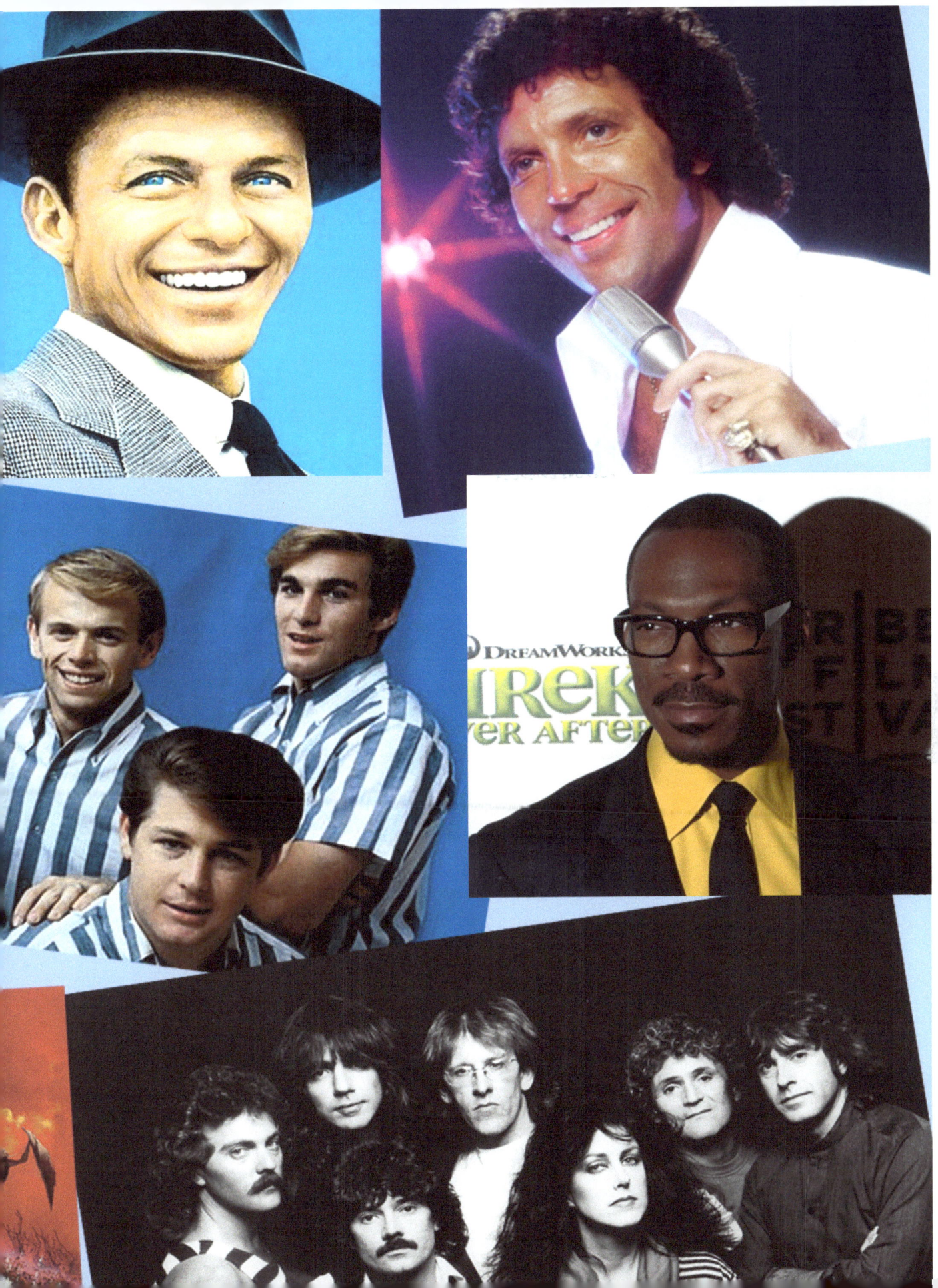

Monica was always advising and helping young writers to get ahead. She found a young actor, Mitch Douglas, whose parents gave him $50.00 to "leave home and find work" when he was just 18 years old. He was later encouraged to leave Kentucky and relocate to New York. Within two weeks he was rehearsing for a tour of *Fiddler On The Roof*. The handsome young actor was looking for opportunities and met Ms. McCall. She saw something in him and felt that he could be the one to take over her clients when she retired. Mitch was reluctant at first to make the move, but he finally agreed. I saw Mitch as a very humble young man, he grew up in Appalachia in a poor community and since I was from the South Bronx and born in a farm in Puerto Rico, we immediately connected with life experiences and became good friends to this day. Mitch spent over 30 years as a literary agent at ICM and in addition to Monica's clients, he also represented other world-famous

Literary and Theatrical Agent Mitch Douglas.

authors like Tennessee Williams and Arthur Miller.

In the theater department, the legendary Audrey Wood, who was just as short and tough as Kay Brown, was the agent who exuded an air of dignity and confidence. She was highly influential in the careers of

Legendary literary agent Audrey Wood was highly influential in the careers of many authors and playwrights including the great Tennessee Williams.

many authors and playwrights including the great Tennessee Williams. The department also included Bridget Aschenberg, who represented playwrights like Lanford Wilson and the creators of original Broadway musicals like *Grease* and *Dreamgirls*, mainly due to Steve Sultan's efforts. Their male counterparts, Milton Goldman and Eric Shepard, represented many of the stars on the Broadway stage like Helen Hayes, Mary Martin, Laurence Olivier, Burt Reynolds, Jon Voight, Faye Dunaway, and my favorite, Chita Rivera.

In the publication arena, Phyllis Jackson and Roberta Pryor had an enormous list of famous authors that included Theodor Geisel, better known as *Dr. Seuss*, Nathaniel Benchley, and his son Peter Benchley, the author of *Jaws*. Many of these agents were getting old and we began to hire new agents like Esther Newberg, who had been involved in politics and worked for Bobby Kennedy during the 1968 presidential campaign. Esther became one of the most powerful literary agents in the world.

Literary agent Esther Newberg.

Broadway Theatrical Agent Milton Goldman.

I was in awe when I first met international stars like Richard Burton, Elizabeth Taylor and other great film stars represented by Paul Rosen. Paul was the head of the motion picture department and a likable fun person with great connections. Included in his department was the young and handsome talent agent Ed Limato, who had been Franco Zeffirelli's assistant and many years later became a powerhouse in Hollywood.

After the first six months running the finances of the company, I noticed a bothersome trend. Some of our main expenses, such as salaries, entertainment, and travel were going sky high and way over budget. My thinking was that the company was employing too many people in all departments, who were doing the same thing and therefore, a reduction in staff was necessary. I met with Marvin and Bob Chuck and told them "We need a restructuring to reduce our expenses and increase our cash

DON COOPER, seated, center, Roulette artist, displays his new LP to, left to right, seated, personal manager Pete Shanaberg and agent Ron Rainey, and standing, left to right, IFA executives Ed Rubin, Ralph Mann, Jeff Dinofer and Andy Kaufman.

JULY 25, 1970, **BILLBOARD**

reserves if we are taking the company to the next level." A few months later, Karl Honeystein, who was a major executive for AFA, resigned and went to Hollywood as a television producer. With Ralph Mann now in charge, I believe Karl felt demoted of his responsibilities. This gave us the opportunity

Motion Picture Agent Ed Limato flanked by two of his clients, Denzel Washington and Mel Gibson, at a screening in 2007.

Attorney Paul Lichtman going out to the West Coast.

to make changes in many departments including a decision to terminate the employment of over thirty employees just before the Christmas holidays. This decision made me feel lousy, but I felt we had to do it. We had lawyers all over the company who were either talent agents or in the business affairs department and among them was Paul Lichtman, who was one of the casualties. Paul was born in The Bronx and went to the famous school for super bright kids, the Bronx High School of Science; and was a Columbia University Law School graduate. As Bronxites, we immediately connected. He was funny, smart, witty and I always felt that he wanted to be a comedy writer and not a lawyer. Despite the short time we worked together, we managed to maintain a long-lasting friendship and business relationship.

The company had old accounting and operating systems, and we encountered many problems regarding the accuracy of the company's records. It felt like we were still in the financial world of the 1950s, so my first task was to implement a new state-of-the-art computerized system. I was familiar with the IBM 714 punch card system that I was trained on at Price Waterhouse and felt confident that it would work for us. Marvin asked me, "How much is this going to cost" and I said, "At least a million dollars". I could see his eyes opening wide, but he approved it. With the help of Joe Loftus at

Price Waterhouse and my team, we were able to implement the change in less than two years. What a great accomplishment to keep track of all the earnings by our clients from the different fields in entertainment like television packaging income, motion picture royalties, commercials on radio and TV, the Rock & Roll department, legitimate theatre, publishing income, and personal appearances. This was the information that Marvin and I needed to determine our cash flow position at any given time to make acquisitions. In the article, *Super-Agent Strikes Again* in the New York Times on June 26, 1977, they write "I C M has a set of computer runs that provide management with at-a-glance readings on the state of the company……" The newspaper article confirmed that the major investment we made in the computer system was a wise move.

Super-Agent Strikes Again

By EDEN ROSS LIPSON

When Henry A. Kissinger was calculating how to turn his years in Washington into a commercial success after leaving the Government, his friends Robert Evans, the film producer, and Barry Diller, chairman of Paramount Pictures, advised him to hire an agent.

They sent him to a slight, trim, freckle-faced man of 50, Marvin Josephson. True to his image for thoroughness, Dr. Kissinger interviewed Mr. Josephson four times before hiring him.

"I worked out the plan alone," said Mr. Josephson, speaking with the rounded vowels of his native Atlantic City, "and it came out on the button."

Mr. Josephson's worldwide sale of Henry Kissinger, media star, included a multimillion-dollar contract with the Little, Brown subsidiary of Time Inc. to publish the American edition of Dr. Kissinger's still-unwritten memoirs, the separate sale of foreign book and serial rights, plus a five-year, $2.1 million contract for personal appearances on NBC television.

The total value of Mr. Josephson's negotiations on behalf of the former Secretary of State is said to be around $5 million—of which Marvin Josephson Associates will receive the standard agent's fee of 10 percent.

Marvin Josephson Associates is a curious publicly owned company—a personal service business that manufactures nothing and has no inventory to warehouse. But it has a tremendous cash flow from contracts that may produce income for decades.

Last year the company grossed $28 million and netted $3.7 million, and in the fiscal year ending June 30 it will do even better. Its principal subsidiary is International Creative Management, a giant talent agency with offices in New York, Las Vegas, Los Angeles, Miami, Rome and Paris and a roster of clients that reads like a Who's Who of show business and the media.

The I.C.M. stable includes Woody Allen, Shirley MacLaine, Tony Orlando, Sean Connery, Peter Benchley, Tennessee Williams, John Chancellor, Harry Reasoner, Tom Jones, Engelbert Humperdinck, Olivia Newton-John, Linda Ronstadt, Fleetwood Mac, Zero Mostel, Peter Sellers, Fay Dunaway, Barbra Streisand and many others.

I.C.M., as it is known by the super stars who use its many-faceted services, has only one competitor in size, the privately owned William Morris Agency, and the two are estimated to handle 15 percent of the active talent in films, television and popular music and a somewhat higher percentage of the very top names.

Mr. Josephson, who is president and chief executive officer of the parent company, personally handles only two clients these days—Steve McQueen and Dr. Kissinger. But I.C.M. offers its services to more than 2,000 other clients.

For Sir Laurence Olivier, now Lord Olivier, that means film, television and commercial contracts. For Michael Crichton, that means books, film-directing and script-writing assignments. For the Captain and Tennille singing team, that means television, nightclubs and concert appearances.

The New York Times
Marvin Josephson

The profits of an agent are restricted to that standard 10 percent of its clients' income from films, book contracts, concerts and the like—but in an unlimited number of deals. Thus, Josephson Associates through I.C.M. had 10 percent of 53¾ percent of the profits of "Jaws," because it represented the producers, the director, the writer and the screenwriter.

It is estimated that the Josephson take from "Jaws" alone so far has amounted to $4 million to $5 million, and the company has similar indirect interests in many other films. A few weeks ago the company's stock climbed in the over-the-counter market because first projections indicated that "Star Wars" may rival "Jaws." I.C.M. represented George Lucas, the writer-director, who had 40 percent of the profits of the film.

Marvin Josephson is a graduate of the New York University Law School who began his career at CBS as a lawyer in the contract section. He did not deal directly with talent there and left to become an independent agent.

Among his first clients was Robert Keeshan (Captain Kangaroo) who, years later, folded his production company into Marvin Josephson Associates, where it remains today as a wholly owned and highly profitable subsidiary.

Another subsidiary is Chasin-Park-Citron in Los Angeles, which is a packager of shows and a smaller version of I.C.M. with a very selective list of clients primarily in motion pictures and television, including Dean Martin, Charlton Heston and Alfred Hitchcock. But I.C.M. accounts for the largest part of the business of Josephson Associates.

Because agents are prohibited by various union rules and state licensing regulations from directly investing in film productions themselves, they cannot usually be involved in the risk capital aspect of the motion picture business.

An exception is the Josephson ownership of the "Captain Kangaroo" chil-

Continued on page 5

New York Times article on June 26, 1977 featuring Marvin Josephson.

Vintage Vending Machine.

Chapter II

Playing with the Numbers

The talent agency was now running smoothly, and everyone felt like one big successful and happy family with over 2,000 clients. The 10% from each client was like a "cash cow" with money coming from every department. Now it was time to play with the numbers.

While I was at Price Waterhouse, one of the clients was having tax issues with the IRS and the client was advised to take advantage of a legal tax scheme to greatly reduce their IRS tax liability. I wondered whether we could use the same concept. Under IRS rules at the time, corporations could depreciate, what was known as *Goodwill* for tax purposes to reduce their tax liability. I called Joe Loftus at Price Waterhouse and reminded him of the famous ABC Vending Machine case, known in the financial world as *"Playing with the numbers"*. He said. "Do you have enough evidence to prove your case?" That was the key question, but my gut feeling was that I was onto something.

Let me try and explain the importance of a company's *Goodwill*. When one company buys another company, goodwill arises when you pay more than what the company's hard tangible assets are worth, like furniture, fixtures and real estate. The amount that is paid above the hard assets is goodwill and it is often difficult to put a value on it. But in our case, I argued that the goodwill was the client list, which although an intangible asset, had been generating revenues for over twenty years.

When Marvin acquired AFA, he negotiated a ten-year loan agreement with Chase Manhattan Bank and two insurance companies. The loan was secured by the assets of the combined agencies as collateral, which of course included the client list. Since the bank accepted the list as collateral, what was the value of the list? This was the tricky part. After a few months of researching the company's revenue-generating history, we were able to put a value on the client list at over $20 million and all the other physical assets at $2 million.

To prove the point to the IRS, we selected the famous actor Burt Lancaster and five other international movie stars as examples. We gave the IRS records showing revenues they had generated in the past and the ability of these personalities to generate major revenues in the future. The majority of clients had been with the agency for over twenty years and the likelihood that they could generate multi-millions of dollars in the future was enormous. The IRS accepted our argument and we were allowed to do the write-off. This allowed us to deduct the entire purchase price of $12.5 million for tax purposes. Our cash reserves went sky high and we began to repay the bank loans, to the extent that we were able to pay off the debt three years in advance.

My accounting team did a fantastic job in gathering the documentation and we all celebrated after the IRS approved the write-off. A week later, Marvin called me into his office and told me "You and your department have done a great job and we would like to appoint you Vice President of Finance for IFA and the new Treasurer of MJA." I thought to myself, "Wow, I broke the glass ceiling, a Latino was now a real team player in the higher echelon of management." I was thrilled.

The promotion came with many benefits that included a nice increase in salary, an expense account, a company car with parking on 53rd Street and Broadway, a parking spot next to one of my favorite dance places, Casa Blanca, on 52nd Street and La Maganet on 53rd Street and Third Avenue that my buddy Tony Rodriguez promoted. It also included the use of the company's apartment across the street from the office. I felt good about myself, more accepted in the company, and my confidence in my abilities grew stronger.

My business card at
Marvin Josephson Associates, Inc .

Chapter III

London and Joyful Paris

One of my many dreams as a young kid was to visit London and Paris, two cities in Europe that I had read about, and they fascinated me. I went to see Marvin and said to him "Our European offices are not generating enough revenues to meet their expenses and I need to see the operations for myself." He said to me, "I'll call Laurie Evans and let him know that you want to meet everyone in the office and about possible changes that we need to make in Paris." That cleared the way for me to go to Europe and come back with a plan. Flying first class on a Boeing 747, known as the "Jumbo Jet" to my first stop in London was an unforgettable experience.

The 1st Class lounge of a 747 Jumbo Jet with a spiral staircase to the bar.

I was met by a "chauffeur" who welcomed me and took my bags. He led me to a beautiful Rolls Royce and I was super impressed with the service. But I also realized that the agents were living lavishly, and we were paying for their lifestyles.

Laurence Evans, the head of all the European offices, was waiting for me along with the entire staff. He was very British in his ways and well dressed. I had little information about Laurie other than he was a shrewd and gentle agent to stars like Albert Finney, Sir John Gielgud, Alec Guinness, Rex Harrison, Vivien Leigh, and Sir Ralph Richardson. His best friend was the great Sir Laurence Oliver. In one of our conversations I asked him, "How did you get to become a talent agent?" and he told me a wonderful story. When he was about 20 years old, he went to Hollywood and had a great time, but he spent his entire family inheritance. He returned to London and in the early 1940s he began to work at Denham studios, where he met Laurence Oliver. They went on a tour of a play in America and when the tour ended in New York, he decided to stay. He then went to California and met Taft Schreiber at the powerful MCA agency and in a conversation, Laurie told him that he wanted to become an agent. He said Taft answered that he was "Glad to hear it, but it's going to take some time for you to learn

My first time in a Rolls Royce… Pure luxury.

about this town. We are looking to open an office in London, are you interested?" Laurie said to me, "I've been here now 25 years." Everyone had the impression that he would be knighted by the Queen, but it never happened.

The next morning, I told Laurie that I was taking a day off to explore London on my own. I began by taking a tour bus and making notes to come back later to learn more about iconic places like Big Ben, Westminster Abby, London Bridge, Buckingham Palace and the Tower of London. At night, the streets of London become even more vibrant and beautiful and I discovered many types of British foods and delicacies like shepherds' pie and the best tasting fresh oysters I had ever had.

The iconic London skyline.

The Palace of Versailles.

After a few days of reviewing the operations, I had enough information. My next stop was the Paris office in the heart of the famous *Avenue des Champs-Élysées*. On the evening of my arrival, I went for a walk and stopped at a small Café. I looked for a sidewalk table and sat looking down the Avenue. At night it was the most beautiful place in the world, another paradise and I realized immediately why Paris is called *"The City of Lights."*

Paris is an expensive city and the office was not generating enough money to cover its costs. I felt it was mainly being used to service the American and British talent when they came to France. The main agent that I wanted to meet was Esther Freifeld, who was always traveling throughout Europe and I asked why? I was told it was because "she speaks six or seven languages fluently and needs to be at all the film festivals throughout Europe to generate business." I was not happy that she was not available, but it was fine because it allowed me to spend the next three days discovering the city.

During my high school and college days, I studied French, so naturally Paris was a destination that I dreamed about visiting. Before I left on my trip, I bought a small pocket size French and English dictionary and made a list of the places to visit. Of course, it was not possible to see everything in the short time that I had. So, I opted to see the places that were iconic, like the Eiffel Tower, the Louvre Museum (*Musee du Louvre*), the *Arc de Triomphe* and the *Cathedrale de Notre Dame*. The history and architecture of each place can only be appreciated by being there and touching, it was an experience beyond words. Paris had a wonderful Hop-On Hop-Off bus tour and I was able to visit all these sites with ease.

I had heard many negative stories about the French people in Paris and how they treated Americans, however I felt very comfortable because I could speak a little French and of course good Spanish. So, when they asked me *"D'où Venez-vous?"* (Where are you from?), I would answer, Puerto Rico, and they were intrigued because I did not say that I was American and spoke with them in Spanish and my little French. They treated me wonderfully, I made new friends and had lots of fun everywhere I went.

One of my favorite historical novels is *A Tale of Two Cities*, by the famous British author, Charles Dickens, a story that takes place in London and Paris before and during the French Revolution of the 1790s. In high school, I read many stories about the French Revolution, King Louis XVI, and Queen Marie Antoinette, who lived opulent lives in the Palace of Versailles, before they were sent to the *guillotine,* where they were beheaded during the French Reign of Terror. Versailles was less than an hour from Paris and I decided to visit the historic Palace. I hopped on a tour bus and spent almost the entire day enjoying beautiful gardens with statues from ancient times and roaming around the 700 rooms with more than 1,000 chimneys. My favorite room was the *Hall of Mirrors*.

Souvenir Post Card of places I visited.

Chapter IV
Going Public Through the Back Door

IFA began to accumulate lots of cash and Marvin asked me to join him at a New York Giants football game to talk about what to do with the extra money. It was also an opportunity for both of us to spend time with our sons; he would bring his son Joseph, and I would bring my son, Andy. The two kids had great times together and it became a normal routine for us to get together in this way practice when we needed to strategize about decisions to grow the company. Marvin said to me "The insurance company in Boston that was involved in lending us the funds to buy AFA, needs to sell off a group of radio stations that they acquired from the owners who defaulted on their loans, and I want to make an offer to buy them." I said to him that the idea was terrific and asked him if Bob Chuck had reviewed the proposed transaction to determine whether there was a conflict in owning a talent agency and radio stations. He told me that Bob and our corporate lawyers had reviewed the issue and in their opinion there was no conflict. I then said to him, "This is great news, the purchase of the radio stations will give us additional credibility on Wall Street."

Marvin kept searching for new acquisitions and the opportunity to represent major sports personalities came when we bought the company owned by Robert J. Woolf, who was a sports lawyer and considered one of the most important sports agents in professional sports. He then went to Los Angeles and made a deal to buy a small elite company, the Chasin-Park-Citron theatrical agency that represented great movie stars like Cary Grant, Grace Kelly, Gregory Peck and Jimmy Stewart, to name a few.

MJA now had five subsidiaries and I was super busy overseeing the financial operations of each company. I had a hectic schedule traveling between New York, Los Angeles, the radio stations and Europe, but I got to do more as well and visit other sites a bit more off the beaten track. I looked forward to visiting the radio stations near Virginia Beach every three months. When you walk on the boardwalk of Virginia Beach, you can hardly see the end of it. It stretches for about three miles along the oceanfront and it reminded me of the beaches in Puerto Rico. One day I took a long walk and discovered that the British had settled in the area in the early 1600s. As a history buff, the whole experience for me was educational and I had lots of fun interacting with the local shop owners.

We hired a top public relations firm to put out the word about the success of MJA to the financial news media. I felt confident that we were on our way to becoming a public company and the publicity would be helpful. But taking a company public to issue stock is a very expensive process so after much research and many meetings, we found a way to substantially reduce the cost by acquiring an existing small public company listed on the over-the-counter stock exchange Pink Sheets and merge them into one. This was called "going public through the back door".

Marvin got word from his contacts on Wall Street that Freddie Fields, the co-founder of Creative Management Associates (CMA), our major competitor and a publicly traded company on the "over-the-counter" stock exchange, was considering selling the talent agency to move into the film production business.

We met with Freddie and his team on numerous occasions before a deal was formalized and finally the selling price was set at about $6 per share. Now we had to find a way to get the money to pay for the shares. Luckily, we had a great relationship with the Chase Manhattan Bank. The money that Marvin had borrowed to acquire AFA was paid back three years ahead of time, a major plus for us. Marvin and I negotiated with the Chase Manhattan Bank for a loan and we made an offer to buy all the outstanding shares of the CMA stock. The bank now saw Marvin as a major player in Hollywood with great opportunities for Chase to get clients. But on the day that we were to sign the purchase agreement, Freddie demanded more money for the stock. Marvin and I were shocked. We went out of the room and checked the current stock price on the Pink Sheets and saw that the price was about 10 cents higher than our bid. We went back in and offered eleven cents more and said we were not going to pay more than the current market value. Freddie was happy with our offer and it was a crazy day, but we acquired our major competitor and overnight, became a major force in the international talent agency business. With the merger of IFA and CMA, International Creative Management – I C M, the behemoth subsidiary of the now public entity, Josephson International Inc. was created on January 1, 1975. We came on the scene with over $200 million in revenues and about 125 agents, second only to the famous William Morris Agency.

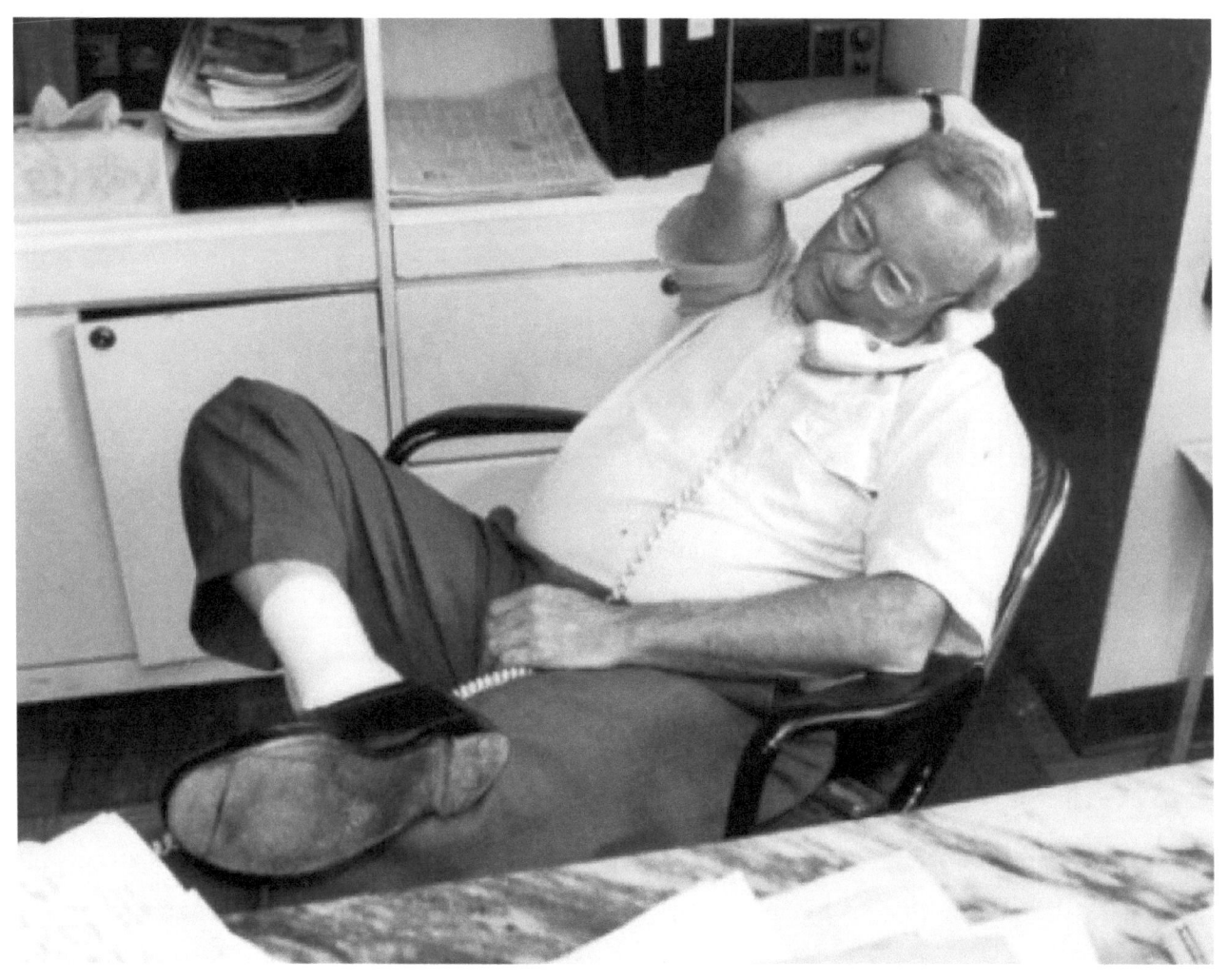

Chapter V
The Art of Movie Packaging

For me, the marriage between the two talent agencies was perfect. CMA controlled the movie packaging business in Hollywood and IFA was the leading television packaging agency in New York. I knew that it was not going to be easy to bring all the characters together and began to do my usual research. Freddie Fields grew up in show business and everyone knew that he was the brother of the famous band leader Shep Fields. He and David Begelman founded CMA and together pioneered the movie "package." This occurs when the talent agency puts a number of their stars, directors and writers together in a single movie project and they became major movers and shakers in Hollywood. Freddie was also a partner in the production company First Artists, whose partners included Paul Newman, Steve McQueen, Dustin Hoffman, Sidney Poitier and Barbara Streisand. Some of the

Opposite page: Super Talent Agent Sam Cohn, Top: Motion Picture Talent Agent Ben Benjamin. Bottom: Television Agent and Hollywood Power Broker Jeff Berg.

packages that he put together included *Butch Cassidy and the Sundance Kid, American Graffiti* and *Star Wars.* Word on the street was that he had developed numerous agents to be super stars like Sue Mengers, Mike Medavoy, Jeffrey Berg and Sam Cohn.

The client list of these agents was a who's who in the industry and included Judy Garland, Woody Allen, Henry Fonda, Marilyn Monroe, Robert Redford, Peter Sellers, Stephen Spielberg, George Lucas and all of the stars connected to First Artists productions.

A couple of months after the merger, I took a trip to Los Angeles to introduce myself to the staff and other members of Freddie's team. Freddie was known to have a lavish life style and I understood the reason. He had married a former Miss Universe and was now married to the famous actress Polly Bergen. I could see that he loved life and happy to go into production, a month later he left the office and I never saw him again.

Whenever a big merger takes place in Hollywood, there is always some disenchantment with who goes and who stays. Jeff Berg was the president of CMA when we merged, and he became the head of the I C M Los Angeles office. I had very little contact with him, but I could see that he was very much like Marvin, full of ambition and I'm glad because he became a major deal maker and earned millions of dollars for the company.

The powerful and demanding talent agent Sam Cohn, who played a major role at CMA, became the head of numerous departments in the New York office. I found him to be a really

Motion Picture Talent Agent Sue Mengers and her young client Anthony Perkins.

strange character; he always wore white socks and chewed tissue paper at meetings and while on the telephone, always had a foot on top of his desk. He was the agent responsible for some of the most famous stars at the time that included Woody Allen, Robin Williams, Mike Nichols, Bob Fosse, Lilly Tomlin and Meryl Streep.

He was a lawyer who had worked at CBS and was the lead attorney at the talent agency General Artists Corporation (GAC), and also became a television producer. He was notorious for not returning people's calls and that pissed me off. Our meetings usually took place at his favorite meeting place, the Russian Tea Room, which is how I met my favorite artist, Salvador Dali, via a Sam introduction and I was in awe. In my opinion, he was the kind of person who felt he knew it all, and therefore it was not easy to get along with him. When I needed to get revenue projections from him, at first, he refused, and I had to keep hounding him. If I told him to control his spending, he would ignore me, and I would let Ralph Mann or Marvin handle it. We had our bouts on many occasions, but we respected each other and always found a way to move on. He was not fond of the Hollywood scene, he would say to me that the people there were plastic and had no culture.

Time Magazine and other tabloids had done articles about Sue Mengers and her clients, and she was featured on a *60 Minutes* segment. Many people disliked her and called her a "flesh peddler," however, she was adored by her long list of clients who included Barbra Streisand, Ryan O'Neil, and Gene Hackman. I liked Sue and thought she had a wonderful sense of humor. Most important to me was that her negotiating skills brought in contracts for millions of dollars. She was a powerful agent and she made sure you knew it. After a meeting that she had with the chairman of Paramount Pictures, Barry Diller, rumors began to circulate that she was looking to leave the company. When Marvin found out, he immediately called me and Bob Chuck to come up with a plan to keep her. I knew that Sue just wanted more money, that was her ploy, "let them think they're missing a hot property", so we offered her a major employment contract that made her one of the most highly paid motion picture agents and sure enough she signed a three-year contract in excess of $200,000 a year.

I also became very friendly with Ben Benjamin, another great motion picture agent. Ben was a very gentle person and we all called him a sweetheart. The first time we met in his office in Los Angeles, he had the film posters of some of my favorite movies, including *Joan of Arc*. He represented Ingrid Bergman and when I told him about my first movie experience, he went to the wall, removed the poster and handed it to me. He said to me… "That's a great story so I want you to put this in your office." His other clients included Burt Lancaster and the great British actor, Sir. John Gielgud.

Chapter VI

The Hiring and Training Practices

The young men and women that we hired to become agents, had to start their careers in the mailroom, which we considered our training program. The daily mail was always hand delivered and it gave each of them an opportunity to meet everyone in the company. This experience was key to help them decide which department they wanted to join when an opening arose. In the entertainment industry is "who do you know". This gave me an opportunity to try and open doors for Latinos; we did not have a presence in the agency business. Everyone we hired came to us from within the network of the white world. I began to wonder about diversity and saw something special in my nephew, Joseph Rivera. He had a good gift of gab, loved the music scene and his lack of fear fit the image of an agent. I felt that hiring and developing Latino agents was important and I discussed it with Ralph Mann and Arthur Trefe, the office manager, who agreed. We gave Joseph the opportunity, we hired him, and he did not disappoint me. After that, whenever there was an opening in the company, I made every effort to give Latinos opportunities to interview. One of those was my dear cousin, Maggie Viruet. I always felt that she had a special desire to be successful and she turned out to be an excellent and important member of my team in the finance and accounting departments.

Mentoring young men and women has been a mantra in my life and is always in my thoughts to help others to succeed. I needed someone I could depend on to help me run the financial operations of all the subsidiaries so I hired a young man, Michael Cooperman and when I interviewed him, I knew he could succeed me if I ever left the company. Michael was smart, energetic, eager to learn and became an important member of my financial team. I made sure that he learned his way through the financial maze. He later on succeeded me as CFO and led the company to more financial successes. I felt so proud of him knowing that I shared my knowledge with him to enhance his career.

One memorable and very funny occasion was our celebration of the 70th birthday of Joe Higgins, head of the personal appearance department in New York. Joe was a proud Irishman and former General Artists Corporation (GAC) super-agent with a great sense of humor. We had a number of young agents that included Andy Kaufman, Rob Light and Eddie Micone, who loved to joke around. On his birthday, everyone conspired to set up a meeting for Joe to meet a new, young, up-and-coming singer. At 1 PM, a beautiful blond walked into his office wearing a large mink coat, with very little underneath. Before taking a seat, she took off her coat. We all went hysterical when Joe's eyes opened wide and he just kept his cool as if nothing unusual had happened and wanted to know more about her. What great laughs we had on many occasions with the agents in the music department.

Opposite page, Michael Cooperman. Top, Joseph Rivera, at right, Maggie Viruet.

Chapter VII
The Towering Inferno

With the merger of the two major talent agencies, the office space we leased on Avenue of the Americas and 51st Street became too small. We wanted to stay in the area and our real estate agent found a great location nearby at the Squibb Building at 40 West 57th Street. The only negative was that we had to take two separate floors. We decided that the Executive offices would be on the 18th floor and included the motion pictures, television packaging, commercials and music departments. My office, the finance department, theatre, and publications would be on the 6th floor. In the spring of 1975, we moved into the new office space while the 18th floor was still in the final phase of construction. Normally, buildings in the City have an annual fire drill but because of the ongoing construction, we did not do this. About two weeks later, on a hot summer morning, we were having a meeting in the boardroom on the 18th floor when some of us smelled something burning and realized there was a fire. We heard a lot of commotion out in the halls. There was confusion and I said, "Everyone needs to leave now." I ran out of the office and got into a waiting elevator to go back to my office and on the way down, it automatically stopped on the 10th floor and a loud noise from the fire alarm came on. The doors

Next day New York Times coverage of the fire.

A scene from The Towering Inferno with Steve McQueen – Faye Dunaway and Paul Newman.

opened, everyone got out, and I ran down the stairs to the 6th floor. Marvin was in Los Angeles, so I called him and explained what was going on and he said, "Make sure you help get everyone out and keep me posted every half hour."

The Squibb Building had 33 floors and there was chaos with people running everywhere. Those who had their offices on the upper floors ran up to the roof of the building and started yelling for help. Everyone else ran down the stairs and gathered outside the building. I looked around and did not see any of my colleagues from the 18th floor and the fire engines were all over the place.

I kept looking up to the 18th floor and could see the flames and the heavy black smoke coming out the windows and it was frightening. My friends were trapped in Marvin's huge corner office, which luckily had been built with all the amenities, including a bath and shower room. The intensity of the fire made it impossible to reach the staircase, everyone ran into Marvin's office. The men took off their shirts and soaked them in water from the adjacent bathroom and then stuffed them into the air conditioning ducts to stop the heavy black smoke from coming into the office.

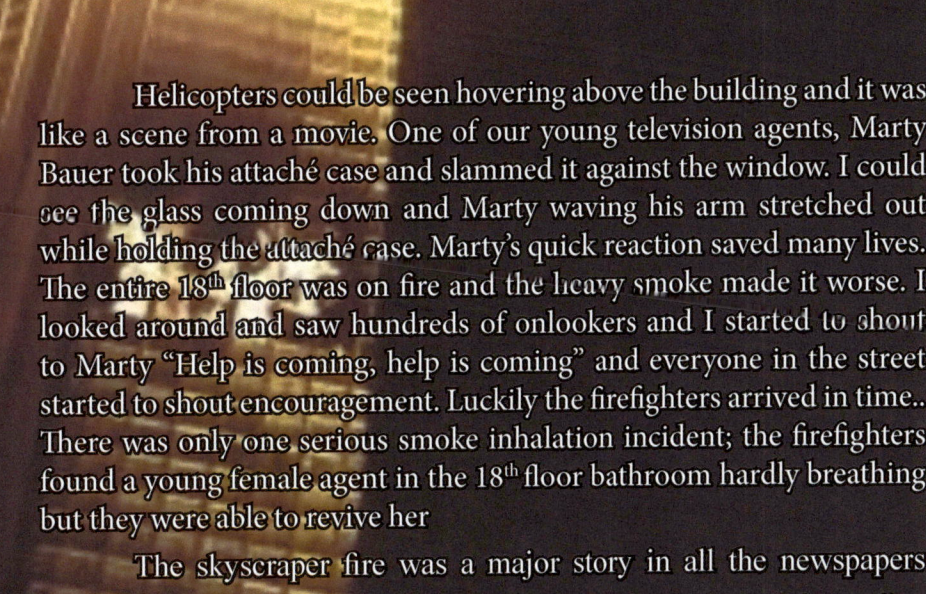

Helicopters could be seen hovering above the building and it was like a scene from a movie. One of our young television agents, Marty Bauer took his attaché case and slammed it against the window. I could see the glass coming down and Marty waving his arm stretched out while holding the attaché case. Marty's quick reaction saved many lives. The entire 18th floor was on fire and the heavy smoke made it worse. I looked around and saw hundreds of onlookers and I started to shout to Marty "Help is coming, help is coming" and everyone in the street started to shout encouragement. Luckily the firefighters arrived in time.. There was only one serious smoke inhalation incident; the firefighters found a young female agent in the 18th floor bathroom hardly breathing but they were able to revive her

The skyscraper fire was a major story in all the newspapers and on television news programs. Ironically, just six months earlier, in December; Twentieth Century Fox released the motion picture *The Towering Inferno* with Steve McQueen and Paul Newman. ICM put together the film package with the two famous actors. As you can imagine, the media had a field day comparing the two events.

Chapter VIII

The 1976 Summer Olympic Games in Montreal

Another one of Marvin Josephson's brilliant ideas was to represent and negotiate the television broadcasting rights for the City of Montreal, which had been awarded the 1976 Summer Olympic Games. He convinced the Mayor that he could negotiate a better licensing agreement with ABC Television. Marvin made a multi-million-dollar broadcasting deal and the Mayor was super grateful and invited Marvin and me to attend the games.

Marvin could not attend and told me to take the family. The excitement that our kids felt when I told them about the trip to the Olympic Games in Montreal was amazing and they went around and told everyone in the neighborhood. My wife Lolly and I decided to make it a vacation with a stop to visit Niagara Falls then drive to Montreal, which was only about six hours away. Queen Elizabeth II attended the opening ceremony on July 17, and we wanted to be there. We began the long drive and only stopped to have food, gas up and made it to Niagara Falls in about seven hours. It was one the most beautiful sites I had ever seen; one could feel the mist and the energy the falls generated.

We stayed overnight at a hotel in Toronto, which was very cosmopolitan and reminded me of downtown Manhattan with similar cityscapes. The following morning, we went sightseeing for a couple of hours and we found the highway that would take us to Montreal. We arrived at the world-famous Fairmont, The Queen Elizabeth Hotel, where the mayor's office had reserved rooms for us. The hotel had all the amenities one can imagine including an Olympic-size pool. It was only a block away from the famous Underground City (*La Ville Souterraine*).

I had heard about this marvelous new style of living in this city and now I was right there, and my curiosity was exploding. The city is mostly underground and is linked to a series of interconnected office towers, hotels, and shopping malls together with residential and commercial complexes. The locals refer to it as Downtown Montreal. It also has a complete underground rapid transit system and when you see it personally, you'll understand why I describe it as an "indoors city."

Opposite page: Beautiful Niagara Falls. Below: The Queen Elizabeth Hotel.

Arrival in Montreal with my wife Lolly and below with my two kids Denise and Andy.

There was a lot of negative news concerning the controversies facing the Olympic Games. Many African nations decided to boycott the games for reasons relating to the apartheid situation in South Africa. The Mayor faced internal problems, and there was also the enormous costs required to put on the event, which were unheard of in the history of the Olympics.

Still, despite the issues relating to the games, my two kids, Lolly, and I will never forget the experience we had. We were given VIP passes to all the events that we wanted to attend, and we were able to see all the important finals in boxing, gymnastics, swimming, track and field, and basketball.

My daughter Denise went wild with happiness when the 14-year-old Nadia Comaneci scored a perfect 10 in gymnastics, a first. She made history when she won three gold medals. She was stunned when she met Monte Hall, the host of the popular game show "Let's Make a Deal." The games were being reported as a battle between the United States and the Soviet Union. The other highlights were in basketball where we witnessed the U.S. Men's team win the gold medal by defeating Yugoslavia. When the U.S. Women's team beat the Soviet Union for the gold medal, pandemonium broke out.

Boxing has always been an exciting sport and the U.S. team was well represented by Sugar Ray Leonard and the Spinks brothers, Leon and Michael. The team won five gold medals. We were in the arena together with people from all over the world waving their countries' flags, and then cheering for the U.S. winners. When I saw them in the ring, it was like magic; you can imagine the confidence in their eyes. They made history as super boxing champions in their respective class.

As the games were being played, one could feel the tension; the Soviets were leading in the medal count and the East Germans were not far behind. The Cuban Teófilo Stevenson won the heavyweight battle and we cheered for him. The Cuban team did very well, they won six gold medals and in track and field, their runner, Alberto Juantorena, was one of the most exciting track and field athletes to watch. I can remember how proud we were when a Puerto Rican boxer won a bronze medal; it was only the second time

The men's Decathlon Olympic winner Bruce Jenner.

a Puerto Rican had won a medal. The first was Juan Evangelista Venegas, a bantamweight, at the 1948 Olympic Games in London. When I laid eyes on Orlando Montalvo, the 1976 bronze medal winner, I saw a young skinny kid with a lot of heart. He was an exciting and feisty person who yelled at me "Muchas gracias!", when we waved our Puerto Rican flag with its one star.

The major moment came when it became apparent that there was going to be a showdown in the decathlon, which is made up of ten grueling events to determine the "World's Greatest Athlete." The contest was between the American Bruce Jenner and Nikolay Avilov of the Soviet Union. Jenner had broken a number of records for points scored. Now it was the final event, and as he came across the finish line, he thrust his arms into the air. Someone who was waving the U.S. flag came out onto the field, and Jenner took it from the person's hand and walked around the track brandishing it. Jenner's win set off an emotional sense of victory and patriotism unlike anything I had ever experienced.

The Soviet Union and the East Germans had very strong teams and we were very proud of our athletes because we came in second in the overall medal count: Soviet Union 125 versus the United States with 94.

Chapter IX

Steve McQueen and the 1968 Ford Mustang GT 390 Fastback

Steve McQueen was one of our premier international clients, earning millions of dollars. His contract had a clause declaring that he would be represented only by the chairman of the board of the agency. McQueen became one of Marvin's priorities and he was now spending a lot of time in Los Angeles to maintain constant contact with him. McQueen was also an established race car driver, loved physical sports and was a karate enthusiast. He invited Marvin to join him in karate lessons and Marvin got hooked with the sport and became close friends with his client.

During the summer of 1977, McQueen, who had not been in a movie since *The Towering Inferno*, came to New York to stay for a while to work on a film project. He asked Marvin to help him find a car, but he wanted to stay under the radar of the news media. I received a call from Marvin and he said: "I want you to come upstairs and meet a client, he needs our help and I told him that I had the perfect person for him." I did not know who the client was, he was dressed very casually, open shirt, jeans, boots, a big beard coving his face and long hair. Marvin said, "Meet Steve McQueen." I was taken back and after chatting for about five minutes he said: "I'm getting ready for a new film role here in New York and while I'm here, I want to see if I can find a 1968 Ford Mustang GT 390 ." My mind immediately went to the film *Bullitt,* where he drove a similar car. I remembered it well because the movie had some of the greatest car chase scenes ever and is considered the most authentic car chase in film history. Marvin then said, "Steve would like to start tomorrow and you can pick him up in front of the building at about 11 in the morning and do whatever it takes to find that car."

The next morning, when he stepped into my car he said, "I have a few friends who tell me that the best place to find it is in New Jersey and the owners usually sell them from their homes." I said to him, "That sounds good, I also was told a similar story by one of my friends who said that we need to drive up and down the suburbs, and it's going to take a while." He then said, "I know, about three years ago, I wanted to the buy the actual one that I drove in the movie, but the owner did not want to sell it and I offered him three times what it was worth."

We began our journey and he kept test driving for about a month. One could see that he was not pleased with any of the first cars we saw. I had to attend to my responsibilities at the office and he had to rehearse, so we began to drive around looking for the car once or twice a week. He was a quiet person and I wanted to get to know more about him other than his life as a major action movie star. He told me he was not too happy about a number of things in his life. On the fun side, he said he felt a high when driving the Mustang in the movie and maybe the car he was looking for would give him the same feeling. I asked him about his next film project and I could sense that he was very excited to talk about it. The word in the industry was that McQueen was very difficult to work with and he said to me: "Number one, I'm bored, "Number two, I don't want to make any more action movies. Number three is that I want to make movies together with my wife, Ali McGraw. I now have something that I believe can make me a better actor." That last statement baffled me, but he kept going. "I am playing the lead role in Henrik Ibsen's *An Enemy of the People*, and I'm doing it mainly with my own money. I'm going to own a major piece of the film, I'm the Executive Producer and have the control that I need on the creative side." I totally agreed with him and I saw his passion to take the risk.

As we were passing a small lot with a number of antique cars he said, "That's it!" He was so happy. We did a test drive and he was smiling. You could see his excitement and when we returned, he took out a signed blank check and gave it to the owner. Steve said, "I want to take the car with me now, just write down the amount". We celebrated by stopping at a restaurant and had a great lunch. I never saw him again after that. His new film had a great director, George Schaefer, and the supporting cast was good, but it failed at the box office. The movie was very talkie and I believe it did not resonate with Steve's "bad boy" audience.

Opposite page - Steve McQueen on his motorcycle

Steve McQueen with his new look and director George Schaefer on the set of An Enemy of the People

Chapter XI
Visiting Communist Cuba
The Bombing of Lincoln Center
Havana Jam

When the legendary and world-famous impresario, Sol Hurok, who represented some of the most famous classical artists, passed away, we saw an opportunity to expand the company. His heir apparent, Sheldon Gold, was the new impresario and with his great team, he represented the likes of Mikhail Baryshnikov, Itzhak Perlman, Andres Segovia, YoYo Ma, and other major classical performers. Sheldon was a man with lots of ambition and great ideas. But he was having difficulties with the new owners of Hurok Concerts and was looking to get out. Marvin Josephson took this opportunity to approach him and we made him an offer he could not refuse.

We formed ICM Artists Ltd, a concert and dance management agency with Sheldon as president, allowing him to bring his team of Walter Prude and Lee Lamont with him. They were the three most important executives who had worked for Mr. Hurok.

Sheldon and I strived to make the new subsidiary profitable from the start. Marvin appointed me the lead person to oversee all operations and to come up with ideas and international opportunities that we could implement.

The Cold War between the United States and Russia was at its' height during this period and there was a hostile international atmosphere in regard to communism. Sheldon visited a number of countries behind the Iron Curtain looking for talent to bring to America. He visited China and made a deal to represent the world-famous Peking Opera which would appear in New York in 1980. He then traveled to Moscow where we made a major deal with the Russian minister of culture to have the famous Bolshoi Ballet Company tour in major cities around the country. He said to me "With these presentations I have now fulfilled Sol Hurok's dreams."

I saw ICM Artists as the opportunity to present to audiences in the United States popular Cuban music for the first time in over twenty years. Any financial dealings with Cuba where not allowed and there was a major embargo, the Russians were in control of the island nation and Americans were forbidden to travel there. Sheldon and I discussed the matter and he agreed that Cuba had great talent in the classical arena and exciting popular music artists. I was determined to find a way to get there.

Around March 1978, I called my dear friend Bobby Garcia, who had just become a U.S. Congressman. I explained what we wanted to accomplish, and he said, "The only way to do it is to set up a cultural exchange agreement between the U.S. and Cuba's Communist government. I'll let you know who to contact, to get permission from the State Department." Bobby came through as always and we filed the necessary documents and through his efforts, we got the approval. Sheldon traveled to Cuba, set up the agreement with the minister of culture and we began to showcase some of their most famous classical performers at various locations around the United States, like internationally known ballet dancer Alicia Alonso and classical guitarist Leo Brouwer.

On one of his trips to Havana, Sheldon ran into Rene Lopez, a close friend and well-known Latin music producer and musicologist of Cuban popular music. He had connections to the minister of culture and was looking to record some of their major artists. In conversations with Rene, he confirmed my idea to present popular Cuban music at venues in major cities throughout the US.

We were given permission by the Cuban government but could not fly directly to Havana. We traveled to Ft. Lauderdale and contracted a small private plane that took us to Cuba. We were all excited about getting

Opposite page from the top: Rene Lopez, Shelly Schultz, Ralph Mann and Ralph Rivera looking air sick.

Right: Meeting up with Bruce Lundvall.

Bottom: The Rabbi with Shelley and Ralph Mann.

to see and listen to the various popular artists and decide who we would bring to the United States to perform. The team was made up of Ralph Mann, Shelly Schultz, Rene Lopez and myself. We engaged Rene to help us with logistics and dealing with the red tape we encountered upon entering the communist island. We were escorted everywhere we went by a wonderful man we only knew as Morejon. He and a driver were assigned to us by the minister of culture. He took us to see every genre of Cuban music including an unforgettable evening at the spectacular and famous Tropicana Club. The people we met were very friendly and loved Americans. Tipping was not permitted, but we found ways to thank them for their service secretly. They did not like the Russians and they made sure to tell us all the bad stories about Los Invasores (The Invaders), as they called them.

We were taken to rum factories to taste their vintage aged rums, sightseeing through Old Havana and they were very proud to show us the Ernest Hemingway museum. It was wonderful seeing cars from the 1940s and 50s that were in tiptop shape. Shelly and Ralph asked to be taken to the synagogue to meet the rabbi and naturally we took photos at the steps of the building. A few days

later, we ran into Bruce Lundvall, president of CBS Records. He was looking to put together a major music event combining popular music from both countries. It was a great coincidence; he and Shelly were good friends and Rene had worked with him on several music productions. After numerous conversations with Morejon and Bruce, it was agreed that ICM would provide some of the major talent and CBS Records would provide transportation and production expenses to record the live event.

A short while after we got back, I received word from Rene Lopez that the group of musicians that we want to bring to New York, Orquesta Aragón, Cuba's most famous popular music band was performing in the Dominican Republic. Shelly wanted to see their complete show on stage before committing to presenting them to New York audiences. We traveled to Santo Domingo and stayed at the Hotel Jaragua and Casino for the weekend, where the orchestra was performing. It felt very strange, to see three guards with military uniforms, each carrying a large machine gun, when we were escorted to our rooms. One of the soldiers was

From the top: Orquesta Aragon, Los Papines and Elena Burke.

Opposite page: The beautiful show girls at the famous Tropicana.

stationed outside the elevators and the other two went in opposite directions and stationed themselves by the exit doors to the staircases. The next morning, we asked about the guards and we were informed by the concierge that it was for our protection. We met with Mojeron and he introduced us to Rafael Lay, the orchestra director and all the other musicians that included one of the greatest flutists in the world of Latin music, Richard Egües. It was a fantastic show and Shelly was very happy. We had so much fun with all the musicians and when we were leaving they said to us "We can't wait to go to New York." Everyone was smiling.

Shortly after we got back from Santo Domingo, ICM Artists Ltd., announced to the press that in December 1978 it was presenting Cuban popular music at Avery Fisher Hall in Lincoln Center. The headlines read "Presenting for the first time in twenty years, directly from Havana, La Orchestra Aragon, Los Papines, an amazing group of five percussionists who are brothers and Elena Burke, a revered singer of romantic ballads who has been compared to Ella Fitzgerald."

When the newspapers printed the story that we had made the cultural agreement with Cuba, I began to receive threatening letters from anti-Castro groups. At first, I did not give it much thought,

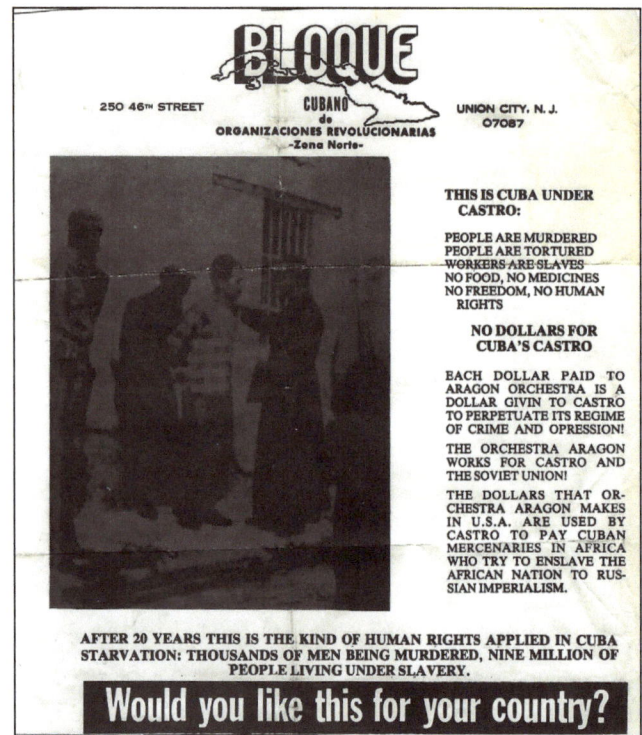

Anti- Castro propaganda that I received in the mail from Omega – 7.

but I informed my colleagues. After getting a number of phone calls and more letters, we decided to tell the FBI and let them look into the matter. Even though it was the New Year's Eve weekend, we scheduled three performances that were sold out beginning with the opening night on Thursday, December 28 and two other shows that followed on Friday, December 29 and Saturday, December 30. The plan was to celebrate the beginning of the new year, and the Cuban musicians wanted to see some of their friends and family that they had not seen in twenty years.

A week prior to the opening, I received a letter that read: "We know where you live so you better cancel the concert." It scared the shit out of me, so I called Bobby Garcia and he arranged for the FBI to increase security. The FBI indicated that an anti-Castro group out of New Jersey, known as Omega-7, was behind the threats and should be taken seriously. On December 28, the FBI posted agents around Lincoln Center and the hotel where the musicians were staying, and the show went on without incident.

The performance at Avery Fisher Hall was a super success; people were dancing in the aisles and Lincoln Center was full of energy with people from all around the world. Many Cubans who attended the event were crying and thanked us for our efforts to bring their musical culture to such a prestigious venue in New York. We were all elated and started counting our profits.

Arrangements had been made to celebrate the success of the first performance at Sardi's Restaurant in the theatre district and after the show, we bussed everyone to the restaurant. We reserved a private room on the second floor and the Cuban Mission had invited many diplomats from various African nations. At about midnight, a waiter came over to me and informed me that I had an urgent phone call. I went to the office and picked up the phone. The person on the other side was a news reporter friend

New York Post Headline.

of mine telling me that both Lincoln Center and the Cuban Mission had been bombed. I could not believe it. I was in shock and immediately rushed back to the table. I whispered to Shelly Gold and the Cuban Ambassador to the United Nations, Raúl Roa-Kourí, what I had just been told. Quick as lightening, the Ambassador clapped his hand three times and there was silence in the room. He said out loud in Spanish that everyone should go back to the buses and return to the hotel at once. No one said a word, but you could feel the tension, and everyone ran to the waiting bus. I called Lolly and told her what had happened, and just in case, asked her to go to our friend, Gilbert Rivera's house for safety. Fortunately, by exploding the bombs late at night, the Omega-7 group wanted to make a political statement, and no one was hurt in the blasts. The damaged caused to the entrance of Lincoln Center was enormous with the floor to ceiling windows and big chandeliers blown to pieces and the two remaining performances were cancelled.

The weekend was a nightmare. Fidel Castro, who had visited New York City and knew the area, insisted that the concert go on, even if on the streets of New York. The weather was very cold,

A cancelled ticket to the concert after the bombing.

— 69 —

but all the artists were ready to perform by the fountain at the iconic Columbus Circle. We spoke with the police and they felt that it could turn into something dangerous, so with the help of Rene Lopez and members of the Cuban community, we were able to find a location on 14th Street, called Casa Las Americas. The meeting place was a New York City base of support for the Cuban revolution. We presented a shorter version of the show for three days, free of charge to the public. After the final performance, we chartered a 747 Jumbo jet to take everyone back to Cuba. The plane was also filled with spare parts for cars, air conditioners and kitchen appliances. The experience was hilarious and frightening at the same time, and after losing $100,000 on the event, we wondered about the next production that we committed to take place in Havana.

Stephen Stills and Larry Harlow from the Fania All Stars.

Jerry Masucci and Billy Joel with the Band Boy at Varadero Beach in Cuba during Havana Jam.

On March 1st, we boarded a chartered Boeing 747 and flew with all the executives, musicians and heavy sound equipment to Havana. We assembled great talent to perform at the Havana Jam at the Karl Marx Theatre. We had an unbelievable week seeing and listening to great music and spending the weekend at world-famous Varadero Beach to enjoy the sun and the beautiful people. The Cuban experience opened up a lot of doors for many years to come.

Johnny Pacheco, Ralph Mercado, Pete "El Conde" Rodriguez and Adalberto Santiago from the Fania All Stars.

Chapter XI

The Writing on the Wall
Going to Hollywood - Life is but a Dream

Marvin was now a major force in the entertainment business and decided to bring new people onto the team, including a new president and make changes to the board of directors as well. At first, I applauded his decision. Our corporate attorney, Alvin H. Schulman, was named as the new president. He was a Yale law school graduate and had a brilliant mind who worked for one of the most prestigious law firms in the country: Paul, Weiss, Rifkind, Wharton and Garrison. John Archibald, another new board member who was a vice president at the Chase Manhattan Bank and a loyal friend, became the new vice chairman.

After Marvin chose his new team, he no longer invited me to events to strategize the way that we originally did on a one-on-one basis. I saw the board of directors was taking the company in another direction by acquiring companies that had no relation to the entertainment field, like a small stock brokerage firm and a furniture manufacturing company. I said to a number of my colleagues, "What the hell do we know about these businesses? I thought we were building an entertainment conglomerate." The new strategy and the acquisitions of these companies were draining ICM's cash reserves.

I understood that we were mainly a talent agency with a few radio stations and limited as to the types of acquisitions we could make. We always had to look hard at the ownership rules that Freddie Fields and Ted Ashley faced. But these new acquisitions were distanced from the entertainment industry. We continued to look for other areas within the industry to grow the company and we saw an opportunity to get into the classical performance business.

There comes a time when you realize that you need to move on and find new opportunities, and I felt uncomfortable with the new direction that Marvin and his new advisors were taking the company. For the first time in over a decade, the idea of looking for a new job was now occupying my mind. I decided that I wanted to get into the physical production side of film and television programs and not just be a numbers guy.

I met a graphics designer and commercial art director, Andy Baltimore, who was also involved in the world of jazz with the great composer, arranger, producer and piano player, Dave Grusin, and

Documentary Filmmaker/Art Director Andy Baltimore and Musician/Producer/Entrepreneur/ Producer Larry Rosen.

producer Larry Rosen. Together they formed the famous jazz label, GRP records. He was working on a documentary about Cañonero, a champion race horse who won the first two legs of the 1971 U.S. Triple Crown, the Kentucky Derby and the Preakness Stakes. I admired his passion for the production process, making sure that the visuals spoke to the audience.

Hanging out with the GRP guys gave me the opportunity to learn another side of jazz, the creative process and they made me feel comfortable. I told them that I had studied and played classical music on the trumpet, but I wanted to learn how to improvise, which is the heart of jazz. I consider them to be among the pioneers of smooth jazz. Working with Andy on several production projects inspired me and the idea that I could also produce documentaries and entertain people was exciting.

The multi-lingual beautiful International Sales Rep Esther Freifeld.

During the summer of 1980, I went to our London office to try and settle tensions among the agents. While having lunch with Esther Freifeld at the famous Ivy restaurant on the West End in the London theatre district, a waiter brought over a bottle of *Dom Perignon Champagne* that we had not ordered. Holding the bottle, he said, "This is a gift from the gentleman sitting at the far end table of the dining room." I looked over and I was very happy to see Irwin Moss, my former colleague from ICM. I went to the table to thank him and he said, "Don't thank me, I want you to meet Sir Lew Grade; he sent the champagne." Lord Grade was an important figure in the entertainment business in Europe and the United States. I thought for a minute, and not wanting to offend him, I asked Irwin, "How do I address him?" Lord Grade replied, "Mi boy, just call me Lew." He continued, "I hear a lot of good things about you and that you are a good business and numbers man. I want you to go to Los Angeles and work your miracles for me." I answered smiling, "Well then, make me an offer I can't refuse." He said that he would be in New York in three to four weeks and would have his office call me to set up a meeting. I went to my table and acting very cool, I told Esther what had just happened, and she said, "That's wonderful Rafael, I want to live in New York and in Hollywood also." I looked at her real strange and smiled.

There were a lot of rumors about Lord Grade and when I returned home, I called my friends to find out more about him and his style of doing business. He controlled ITC Entertainment, a major independent film and television production company with a distribution arm that was losing

The flamboyant British movie mogul Sir Lew Grade.

Announcement in the Hollywood Reporter of my new position as Vice President and CFO of Marbel Arch Productions.

money. My friend Irwin Moss was the head of the television division. He also controlled Marble Arch Productions (MAP), a major independent production company with offices in London, New York, and Los Angeles. Lew had set up a deal with Universal Pictures to distribute his films in the United States.

It was widely known that Lew Grade was famous for bringing *The Muppets Show* and Jim Henson to children's television after all American television networks had turned it down. However, he had recently made some very bad business decisions and his companies were losing money left and right. He was born in the Ukraine and became a British citizen. He started out as a dancer and then a talent agent, and then a big-time producer. I was told by many that he was a great salesman with major ambitions and I admired that about him. The new rumor circulating was that his companies had lost over $80 million in the past two years and he was losing his touch to get more funding for his films.

Lew was a loveable gentleman, in his seventies, when I met him. He had a tremendous ability to talk people into putting up the money for many high-profile productions in motion pictures, theatre, and television programs, that were both successful and profitable. He was considered one of England's greatest impresarios and was knighted by the Queen for his contributions to the nation. Another rumor of his reputation was that sometimes he promised one person one thing and when meeting with the next person, he would agree to proposals that were contrary to the promises he had made earlier. This led to a lot of financial problems for him, beginning in 1980 when his company produced *The Legend of the Lone Ranger* which was a creative and financial disaster and lost $40 million. His company then produced the motion picture *Raise the Titanic* and the film had similar production issues. It was a financial flop and lost nearly $20 million.

Much to his credit, Lew Grade realized that he needed someone like me to turn his companies around and make them profitable. The whole picture became clear to me, I was looking to get out of the mess that was going on at JII/ICM and this was a great opportunity to learn about the physical production of motion pictures. I felt that I was at the right place at the right time. The task was very challenging, but moving to Hollywood was also enticing, and appealed to my adventurous side and I thought to myself, "I need to move on and I can do this."

Sure enough, the following month, Lew's office called me for a lunch meeting with him and Martin Starger, who was president of Marble Arch Productions. We met at our favorite restaurant, where there was always a table reserved for him, the Russian Tea Room. He said that he loved their Chicken Kiev and I told him it was also my favorite, so he ordered for both of us. He said to me, "You want to be a producer?, so this is my offer, you bring in my next two films on budget and if they are profitable, you can be the producer of our third film." I was surprised at the fantastic offer and feeling great about myself, I said to him, "If you agreed to my condition not to override my financial decisions, we have a deal." We all shook hands and a few weeks later I received the employment contract of my life. I was named as the Chief Financial Officer of all Marble Arch film and television productions reporting to Marty Starger and Lord Grade. I saw the move to Hollywood as a beginning of my new career and I wanted to discover if it was true that there was "Gold in them Hills". I was on my way to becoming a Hollywood film producer.

www.ingramcontent.com/pod-product-compliance
Lightning Source LLC
Chambersburg PA
CBHW040735150426
42811CB00063B/1638